MUNGAKA

WORD BOOK

MUNGAKA WORD BOOK

Ŋwà'nì Lɨŋ kɛ̆ nì Mìŋgâkà

Lilian Ndangam Fokwang

Spears Books
Denver, Colorado

Spears Books
An Imprint of Spears Media Press LLC
7830 W. Alameda Ave, Suite 103-247
Denver, CO 80226
United States of America

First published in the United States of America in 2021 by Spears Books
www.spearsmedia.com
info@spearsmedia.com
@spearsbook
Information on this title: www.spearsmedia.com/mungaka-word-book
© 2021 Lilian Ndangam Fokwang
All rights reserved.

No part of this publication may be reproduced, distributed, or transmitted in any form or by any means, including photocopying, recording, or other electronic or mechanical methods, without the prior written permission of the publisher, except in the case of brief quotations embodied in critical reviews and certain other noncommercial uses permitted by copyright law. For permission requests, write to the publisher, addressed "Attention: Permissions Coordinator," at the address above.

ISBN: 9781942876908 (Paperback)

Design and typesetting by Spears Media Press LLC, Denver, CO

Dedication

For my mother Helen Loma Ndangam – my first teacher. Always loving and supportive.

In loving memory of my grand father, Ba David Ndangam – I am because you were. I can because you did.

CONTENTS

Preface ix
Acknowledgements xii
In and Around the House 1
Ma Ndab

Cooking 12
Mà Naŋ Mbaŋ

Buildings and Places 18
Ndabkɛd boà Lɨ'kɛd

School 21
Ndâŋwà'nì

Transportation 24
Kĕ Kǔjìd

Food 26
Kĕjɨ

Insects and Animals 38
Bàtà bô Bànyàm

Nature and Landscape 54
Kɨmvi

Birds 62
Bà Bɨsɨŋ

Dressing 68
Kĕ mà We'

Farm and Hunting 72
Ŋgwɛn boà Vum

People 77
Bòn\Bɨn

Music and Dance 81
Kĕ Wè boà Bɛn

Additional Vocabulary 85
Photo Credits 89
Index 91

PREFACE

One of my fondest memories of growing up is spending Christmas with my grandparents in Tikali, Bali Nyonga. My late grandfather David Ndangam took great delight in teaching us Mungaka (Mìŋâkà) Christian songs. We would spend time rehearsing Christmas choruses which were often used during church services. When anyone sang out of tune or mispronounced a word, my beloved grandfather who was then blind and slightly hard of hearing will pause the rehearsal, gently correct the person, and ask them to repeat the line in the song. After that, we would start singing again while he listened attentively. I enjoyed these lessons as much as I enjoyed spending time with my grandfather whose enthusiasm for the language was evident to anyone who spent time around him. My grandfather had been part of the team of native speakers who assisted in translating the Bible into Mungaka. Years later, as an adult I came to appreciate the monumental effort that translating the Bible into Mungaka had entailed and the extent to which Biblical text had helped paved the way for documenting what had always been an oral culture. My first attempt to read a Bible passage in Mungaka came during the memorial service for my maternal grandfather in 2001 when my sisters and I were tasked with reading the Mungaka Bible during the service which was conducted entirely in Mungaka at the Presbyterian Church Sàŋ. I recall we spent the night before memorizing the respective Bible verses so that we could read these properly and effortlessly in church. That a speaker of a language might not necessarily be able to read and write it, is not new. I grew up speaking Mungaka. However, like many native speakers of the language, I never learned how to read or write it. Throughout my studies, English was the language of instruction. The only Mungaka book available in our house was the Mungaka Bible which I could not read because I was not familiar with the German alphabet on which it was based.

Mungaka is the linguistic description of the language of the Bali Nyonga people of the North West Region of Cameroon with an estimated 500,000 speakers worldwide. Mìŋâkà literally means 'I say'. The endonym of the language is Chû Bà'nì (meaning, the language of Bali people). It is a tonal language which means the meaning of words varies depending on the tone (for instance, *Ba*/father, *bǎ*/the people of/, *bà* -we/us). The language itself evolved from a combination of Mubako (the language spoken by the Bali Chamba who migrated from Northern Cameroon) and some languages from the Western Region of Cameroon, notably Bati. Despite the widespread use of Mungaka as a language of the church in the Cameroon Grassfields during the early 20th century, very few native speakers had a grasp of reading and writing the language. This prevalent illiteracy in the language was made even more challenging by the complexity of the German alphabet on which written Mungaka was based.

However, following completion of the revision of the Mungaka alphabet in 2010 by the Mungaka Rehabilitation Committee, there has been a growing interest in reading and writing Mungaka from native speakers and non-native speakers alike. The launch of the Mungaka 101 in the fall of 2018 and Mungaka 201 in 2020, respectively taught online, provided an ideal opportunity for me to begin learning to read and write the language. Inspired by the scarcity of written resources in Mungaka during my childhood and my growing ability to read and write Mungaka, I set about developing a resource to help with Mungaka vocabulary building because I believe vocabulary is fundamental to learning a language. The availability of didactic resources such as this book make learning a language more practical, realistic, and engaging.

The purpose of this picture book is to enhance language learning for readers by increasing their Mungaka vocabulary competency. The book aims to serve as a resource for vocabulary building that will interest both general readers and native speakers. Non-native speakers and early learners of the language will find it useful in increasing their vocabulary competency, while native speakers will equally find herein, words that will enrich their vocabulary. Beyond vocabulary acquisition, the book also offers readers especially native speakers an opportunity to engage and familiarize themselves with the new standardized Mungaka alphabet. It adds to the growing body of Mungaka language resources aimed at helping both native speakers and beginning learners to learn to read and write the language. Indeed, such a growing interest necessitates the ongoing production of didactic resources to assist with language learning and vocabulary development.

Language is vital to a culture and the identity of its people. To this end, the words and illustrations in the book offers some insight into Bali Nyonga culture and way of life. For instance, the different types of traditional outfits worn by men, the varieties of musical instruments and even the types of calabashes, indicate the symbolic prominence of these in Bali Nyonga cultural heritage. Accordingly, I have tried as much as possible to select illustrations that are socio-culturally relatable and meaningful to native speakers of Mungaka. This was particularly important in the case of animals and birds as some species differ based on their environment. Researching this book was also a sad awakening to the depth of the extinction of animals in the region. For instance, I spent days researching the name of the bird whose red feather is used to recognize notables locally (*ŋguʼ*). I eventually went on to read entire articles about Bannerman's Turaco (*ŋguʼ*) and learned how it had become a threatened specie due to its feathers being used for recognizing notables in several ethnic groups in the region. Similarly, animals like hyena (*gwǎnyìnyi*) and leopard (*ŋgìnyàm*) are now rare to find in the area.

Language and world views are shaped by the society in which the language is spoken. There are concepts in the English language that Mungaka simply has no equivalent for, not because the language is deficient in its vocabulary but because the concept does not or did not exist in the society and world view of the people. In such instances, the language has loaned words from English (e.g., *têbì* for table or *pepà* for paper) or created a word for the concept (e.g., *tàkɨtɨ* for airplane or helicopter). Similarly, there are concepts in Mungaka that are not easily conveyed in the English language. For instance, there are two verbs for "to eat" in Mungaka *(mà kwɛd, mà ji)* and their usage is distinguished contextually by how the food was prepared (boiled, baked or roasted). Words in a language can also represent the world view of the people. For example, in Mungaka, the word *mfɛd* is used to refer to brother, sister, half-sister, half-brother, and cousin. The absence of a distinction between siblings, half-siblings, and cousins in the language, reflects the emphasis on strong family ties within Bali society. I caution readers of this book not to seek the Mungaka equivalent for every noun which exists in the English language. For instance, a giraffe which is found in parts of Northern Cameroon, is not indigenous to the Cameroon Grassfields. Consequently, the Mungaka language does not have a name for giraffe. Regardless, the hope is that the visual clues included here, will enable the non-native speakers and beginning learners alike to engage with both the pictures and the accompanying text in a way that fosters oral language development while simultaneously facilitating, vocabulary building, writing skills and reading through attention to spelling (alphabet and tones). While the photo illustrations in the picture book will help readers understand what they are reading, it is important that the pictures are taken as contextual clues to words. To help with word pronunciations and tones, early learners would benefit from listening to Mungaka words pronounced by native speakers as sounding out the words will help build oral language skills.

As much as possible, the book is organized around themes: from objects around the house, animals, insects, birds to buildings, people, and food. As an extra feature, a list of nouns without pictures is included at the end of the book. These include illnesses, parts of the body, months of the year and familial relationships. It is my hope that between these pages you find a valuable resource for building your Mungaka vocabulary, learning the new Mungaka alphabet and enhancing your fluency in Mungaka.

Aurora, Colorado
November 2021

ACKNOWLEDGEMENTS

This book arose mainly due to my interest in Mungaka language and the culture of the people of Bali Nyonga. I am grateful to my parents Ba Gwanua Ndangam and Ma Helen Ndangam for laying a solid foundation by making sure my siblings and I grew up speaking Mungaka and learning about Bali Nyonga culture. Throughout the compilation of this work, I relied on the knowledge, network, and expertise of so many people for whom I am deeply grateful. My mother patiently sounded out words from the Mungaka dictionary written in the old German inspired alphabet which I still struggle with. She helpfully clarified some concepts and provided guidance whenever I needed it. *The Mungaka Dictionary* compiled by Johannes Stöckle in 1992 served as an instrumental resource. The well researched reference dictionary compiled by Stöckle and his team was immensely valuable.

While it was easy to compile and categorize nouns from the dictionary, the task of researching and finding pictures to characterize these nouns was not easy. I used several free and paid photo resources online including Dreamstime, Pixabay, Pxfuel and Wiki Media Commons. I equally benefitted from the resourcefulness of family members and friends to whom I am grateful: Ba Titamohkumi, Ma Kuna Titamohkumi, Ni Julius Ndangam, Ma Eva Caspa, Ma Juliet Tasama, Ni Gilbert Nyonka, Ma Immaculate Fokwang, Ni Theodore Fokwang and Ni Sema Fofung generously provided some of the pictures featured in the book. For my research on birds that are indigenous to the region, I relied heavily on Avibase – The World Bird Database and Birds of the World Database maintained by the Cornell Lab of Ornithology.

This initiative could not have come about without the support of critical people at key moments in its development. I am grateful to uncle (*Nimbàŋ*) Ni Tita Forsing who was instrumental in identifying the names of musical instruments especially different types of drums in Bali. I equally tapped into his vast and impressive knowledge of birds and animals of the region. I deeply appreciate Ni Godlove Gwaabe for generously responding to my countless inquiries on different concepts within the culture, the nuances of the language and for his editorial feedback; Ni Ferdinand Nteh, a member of the Cameroon Bird Society helpfully provided the names of some birds in English and identified the English name for *mbɨ* (African olives); and Ni Kennedy Nyongbella who enthusiastically answered my questions about some plant species in the region.

The insights shared by my fellow classmates of the Mungaka 201 cohort of 2020/2021 – taught entirely in Mungaka were invaluable during research for this project. Ni Fidelis Kaspa and Ba Pius Sojah were quite resourceful in their contributions respectively shared on our class group. I am forever indebted to my peer reviewers Tita Nyuga Galega, Ma Eva Caspa,

Ma Alice Lima, Ma Faith Fohtung and Ma Irene Tita who respectively reviewed the work and shared detailed feedback.

Lastly, a profound thanks to my husband and editor Jude Fokwang who embraced the project, cheered it, and helped bring it to the world through Spears Books.

In and Around the House
Ma Ndab

Bedroom
Ndânɔ̀ŋnŏŋ

Living room
Tali

Furniture
Yumndab pl. Kĕndab

Tin/can
Tɔ'

Pumice
Wɔsu'kù

Roof
Tundab

Anvil hammer (used by blacksmith)
Ndǔnlàm

Wooden hammer
Mbù'wè / mbù'ghwè

Comb
Sàd

Ceiling
Tăŋndab

Key
Kĕ'fɨn

Toy
Yumtasɪ̀' pl. kĕtasɪ̀'

Photo
Fotò / Kà'a

Bed
Kun

Lamp/light
Mu'

Chair
Lèŋ

Broom
Jə'tì

Box/trunk
Kuŋ

Mirror
Mălàm

basket
Ŋkì'

Window
Tɔ'ndab

Toilet
Kɔ̀d

Nail
Mfam

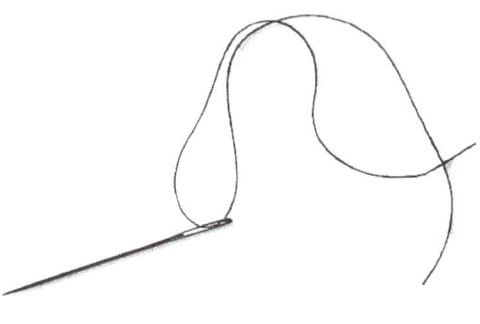
Needle
Njàŋ

Mat
Kè

Cobweb
Ndămndâm

Door
Nchùndab

Soap
Chinji

Razor
Kèm

Clock
Nyùm

Curtain
Njîntâmtam

Gnome
Ŋkwêndɔ̀'

Wall
Mbènndab

Cork
Jè'ni nchəŋ

Ladder
Kɔ'tàŋ

Chewing stick
Sàb

Umbrella
Mândìkàŋ

Table
Têbì/kɨlaŋ

Camwood powder
Bɨ

Rag
Chə̀'ɨ nji

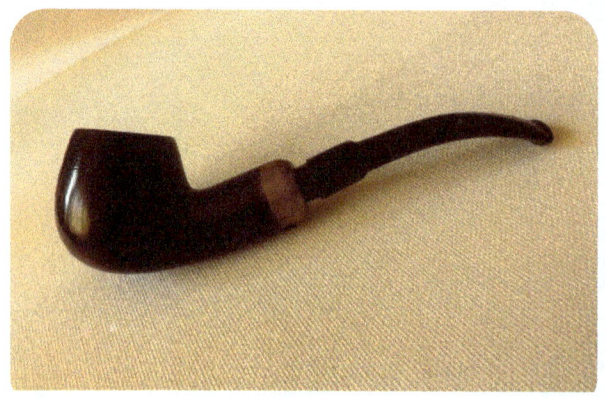

Tobacco pipe
Chĭŋdìbà'

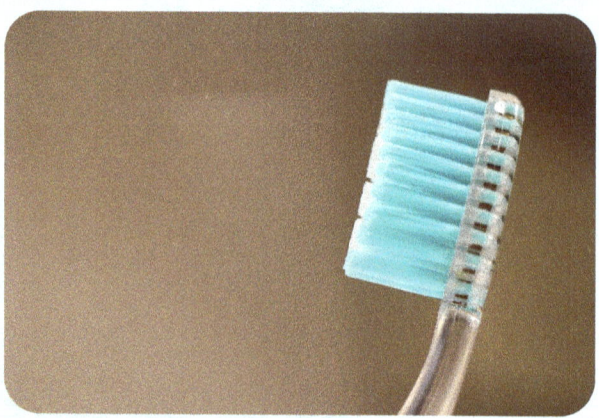

Toothbrush
Sàb

Bottle cover
Kɔbti nchəŋ

Medicine bag
Bămfù

Scissors
Bamtì

Sewing machine
Màsîŋ

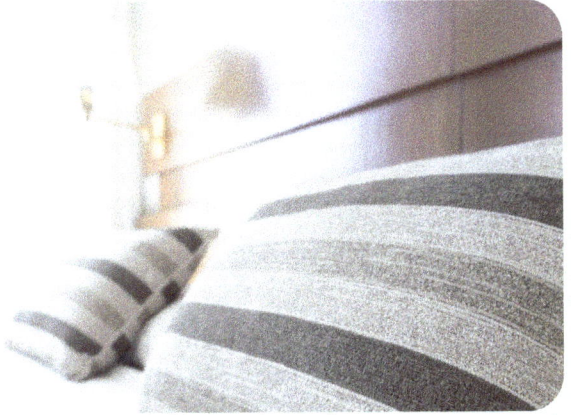
Pillow/cushion
Mbuɲtìkun

Towel
Tawə̀lì

Blanket
Plàŋkɨtɨ

Indian bamboo
Bàŋmfɔ̀'

Small basket often used during dance performance
Ŋgwòn

Thread
Ŋkɨ̀

Basket for carrying chicken & produce
Kà'-ŋgɔb

Horn cup
Ntu'

Calabash for serving palmwine
Lə' ndù'

Calabash used for tapping palm-wine
Bàtì

Money
Ŋkab

Large calabash for storing palm-wine
Ka' ndù'

Telephone
Tɔ'ŋgàm

Stool
Tu'laŋ

Footstool
Yumchi'ti kù

Bamboo stool
Lĕŋ ndə̀ŋ

Whip
Ŋgwàn

Gift
Ŋkèn

Cooking
Mà Naŋ Mbaŋ

Bowl
Kaŋ

Red hot charcoal
Titemu'/ kikemu'

Clay pot
Tàd

Clay Pot for brewing beer
Tăd ŋkaŋ

Clay pot for cooking fufu
Tàd ŋgɨ̀ŋ

Cup
Ntu'

Drink
Ndù'

Fireside
Chěnmu'

Firewood
Ŋkwin

Flat basket for serving food
Kɨ̀kad

Flat calabash
Ghɨbti

Fork
Sɔ̌bnyàm

Grinding stone
Wo tita

Small stone for grinding
Mûndù

Knife
Minyi

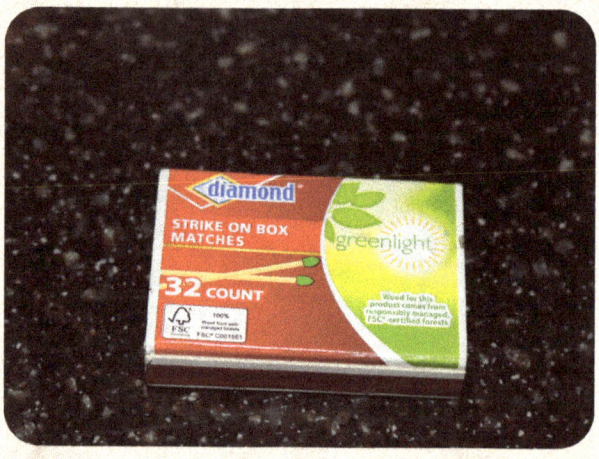
Match sticks
Ŋgwàdmu'

Mortar
Ŋkà'

Funnel
Yădndù'/Jèn

Palm oil
Ŋgwêd bàŋ

Pestle
Ŋkɔ̀ŋ

Plate
Bàbti kaŋ

Pot
Mbaŋ

Ladle
Fɨkəb mà naŋ mbaŋ

Sawdust
Mbɔbtɨ

Sieve
Sèkèlì

Spoon / ladle
Fɨkəb

Stick for cooking fufu
Nkŏŋŋgɨ̀ŋ

Water
Nchì

Wood ash
Bumu'

Bottle
Nchəŋ

Palm kernel husks
Chicha' mbàŋ

Tong
Bamtì

Calabash
Ghə

Black pepper
Nyɨ'sòb

Buildings and Places
Ndabkɛd boà Lɨ̀'kɛd

School
Ndâŋwà'nì

House
Ndab

Church
Ndânyikɔ̀b

Cross
Mbàŋnìmbàŋni

Hospital
Ndâjaŋ

Workplace
Lǐ' fà'

Grave
Tusì

Royal palace
Ntèd

Customs office
Ndâsebkě

Court
Ndâsa' sa'

Market
Ntan

Bookshop
Ndântân-ŋwà'nì

Bathroom
Ndâsǔ'mbùm

Traditional gate
Nchǔ bù'

Town or country
Ŋgòŋ

Prison
Ndâchaŋ

School
Ndâŋwà'nì

Paper
Pepà

School
Ndâŋwà'nì

School yard
Jǔŋwà'nì

Book
Ŋwà'nì

Book cover
Gha' ŋwà'nì

Pencil
Ŋkɔŋŋwà'nì

Pen
Ŋkɔŋŋwà'nì

Bell
Jòŋ/ Njəŋ

Envelope
Bămŋwà'nìntum

Scissors
Bamtì

Dice
Dàg

Students
Ghăŋ-ŋwà'nì

Transportation
Kĕ Kŭjìd

Car
Motò

Bicycle
Băskud

Plane
Tàkɨtɨ

Helicopter
Tàkɨtɨ

Boat
Baŋ

Bridge
Kɔ́'

Road
Mànjì

Wheel
Kalì

Food
Kějɨ

Bitter kola
Ŋgànjòm

Bambara groundnut
Njù

Palm oil fruits
Mbàŋ bàŋ

Peanuts
Mbìyaŋ

Kola nut
Bì

Melon seeds
Njɨ̀'

Bitterleaf
Vub

Cocoyam leaves
Fǔ kǔ'

Cow pea leaves
Wà'

Garden eggs
Nyà'

Okra
Ghɨ̀ghàŋ

Pumkin leaves
Chə̀m

Mushroom
Bɔ̀'

Garden Huckleberry
Sànjàb

Dwarf banana
Lìpə'

Guava
Tamtɨ (Ntamtɨ, pl)

Cape gooseberry
Mɨtìtɔ̀'

Raffia palm fruit
Kǔ'ŋka

African cashew
Ŋga'

African Plums
Jòm

Avocado
Piyà

Bambara ground nut pudding
Njù

Banana leaf
Fǔ-ŋkɨndɔ̀ŋ

Beans
Ŋkun màli

Bread
Ngǐŋ mɩ̀kali

Cassava
Kàsɨŋga

Cocoyam
Kǔ' damàwa'

Coffee
Kɔ̀fi

Corn
Ŋgàfɨd

Corn flour
Bɔŋgìŋ

Country onions (Afrostyrax lepi-dophyllus)
Mùnjù

Dried crayfish
Njàŋgà bàŋ

Egg
Mbǔmŋgɔb

Ginger
Njǎchɔ̀'

Honey
Dù

Honeycomb
Kǎmdù

Malanga
Kǔ'màghàbo/ Kǔ'màghàbà

Peanut pudding
Mbɔ'

Palm wine
Ndǔ'ŋka (wine from raffia palm)
Ndǔ'tən (wine from oil palm)

Pepper
Tita

Plantains
Ŋkɨndòŋ

Potatoes
Jubàŋ

Rice
Ŋkun mɨ̀kali

Salt
Chi

Sugar cane
Ŋini

Cluster yams
Ju' ndɔŋbɨn

Taro root/Achu coco
Mâkǔ' /Kǔ' chu'

Tobacco leaves
Ndìbà'

Yams
Ju'

African olive
Mbɨ

Cameroon aframomum
Chɔ̌'

Alligator pepper
Sù'

Guinea corn
Ngǐŋ ŋkɔ'

Seeds of peace
Nìndɨm

Carrot
Fom

Castor oil plant
Bàndɔŋ

Cocoa
Kokò

Palm kernel
Wɔlɔ' mbàŋ

Corn fufu
Ŋgɨ̀ŋ

Meat (generic)
Nyàm

Corn & groundnut pudding
Sugwà'a

Groundnut soup
Ntò mbìyaŋ

Fermented corn porridge (pap)
Ntòn

Corn pudding
Kɨ̀mbam

Achu soup /yellow soup
Titâ chu'

Large taro root
Kǔ' njâm

Plantain porridge
Ŋkìndòŋ ntatìtati

Colocasia flower (elephant ear)
Ntàŋkǔ'

Egusi soup
Ntò njɨ̌'

Pumkin
Bɔ̌'lam

Insects and Animals
Bàtà bô Bànyàm

Ant
Ngǐŋgàŋ

Bee
Dù

Beetle
Nsɛ̀n

Butterfly
Ghɨha

Poisonous caterpillar
Ntŏmntôm

Caterpillar
Chìchwè

Cockroach
Mbin

Dragonfly
Tămbàlàŋ

Dung beetle
Mɨfù'ti-mbɛd

Field cricket
Tăchì

Firefly
Tɔ̀ŋwidŋwid

Fly
Njĭnjì

Gadfly (big mosquito)
Nchuŋ

Grasshopper
Ŋgɛ̀n

Small beetles
Kɨmfemfe

Lice
Ntĕd

Maggot
Tìd

Locusts
Ŋgɨm

Millipede
Ŋgɔ̀ŋnìkɨb

Mosquito
Lĭlì

Moth
Dumɨ

Mygale blondi spider
Ŋgâmnsi

Spider
Ndămndâm

Stink bug
Làmnchuŋchuŋ

Termite
Ŋgɔ'

Wasp
Ŋkônfɨn

Weevil
Mfù'

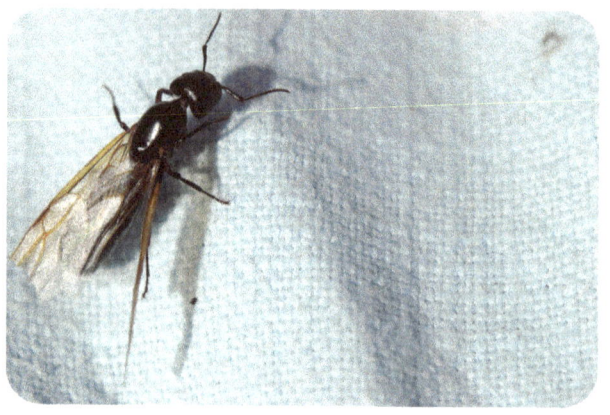

Small winged ant
Mɨse'ninsɔ̀ŋ

African civet
Chɔ̆bnyàm

African forest Buffalo
Nyad

African ground squirrel
Kàŋmbùn

Agama lizard
Bŭ'ninduŋ

House cricket
Tămchicha'

Small grasshopper
Sɨŋŋkà'

Animal horn
Ndɔŋ

Shrew mouse
Sòŋbulùŋ

Antelope
Ŋgab

Armadillo
Ŋgăŋgâ'nyàm

Bat
Ləm

Boa constrictor
Ŋgɔbnyo

Buffalo horn
Ndɔ̂ŋnyad

Cameroon clawless otter
Bulùŋ

Cat
Mɨnyàŋgɔb

Chameleon
Ŋkɔŋnìndàm

Chimpanzee
Bùbu'

Baboon
Mbìchɔ̀'

Cow
Nyàmnchì

Crocodile
Ŋgàn

Cane rat
Njə̀bɨ̀

Ram
Làŋ

Dog
Mvɨ

Elephant
Nswen

Field rat
Mbǎbndìn

Fish
Nsu

Frog
Tàmnsòn

Goat
Mbi

Guinea pig
Mbɔ'mbàb

Hedgehog
Ŋgǔbnyàm

Hippopotamus
Nìŋgwàn/ Ndìŋgwàn

Horse
Nyàmbà'nì

Hyena
Gwǎnyìnyi

Leopard
Ŋgìnyàm/ŋgì

Lion
Bu'mbèn

Lizard
Kùbkùb

Deer
Mɨchì

Wild boar /Forest hog
Kunyàm kɔ̀b

Monkey
Ŋkan

Mouse
Mbàb

Ox
Mfɔ̀ŋ

Pig
Kunyàm

Porcupine
Nyàmnjɔŋ

Pygmy elephant
Mɨmbǐ

Python
Ŋgɔbnyo

Rabbit
Nìnjɘ̂m

Kid
Mbîŋkə'

Red palm weevil
Mvən

Royal antelope
Musid

Shad fish
Ncha

Sheep
Njə̀mbi

Reedbuck
Ŋgì

Small black fox
Mbìnyàm

Snail
Tà'ndùŋ

Snake
Nyo

Squirrel
Jùjùsaŋ

Fish otter
Bulùŋ

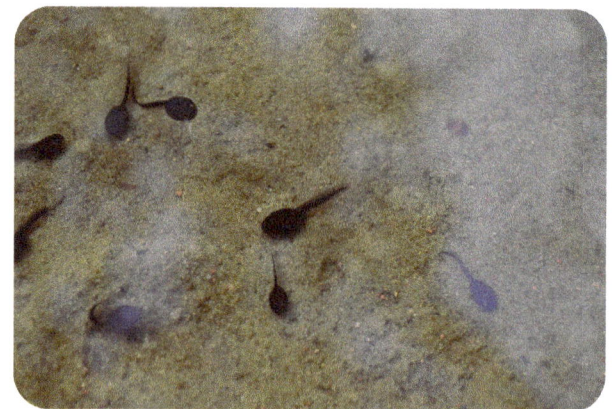
Tadpole, small fish
Lɨ

Toad
Tìtɔ̀'

Tortoise
Kimàŋkɔ̀'

Water snake
Ndàmnchì

Waterbuck
Njwǎ

White field mouse
Fufù

Wood worm
Ŋkɔ̀'nìtɨ

Nature and Landscape
Kɨmvi

Cave
Ŋgɔ̀'

Cloud
Mìmbà'

Crescent
Gha'ŋu

Dust
Mbɔ̂mncha'

Fine sand
Sàn san

Fog
Fu'tu

Forest
Kɔ̀b

Grassland
Ŋkònŋkà

Hill
Mbad

Hole
Bɔ'

Lake
Wètèla

Lightning or thunder
Făŋmbɨŋ

Moon
Ŋu

Mountain chain
Mbadndàlì

Mountain
Mbad

Mountain or hill slope
Ŋkwa mbad / mbènmbad

Mountain peak
Nchămbad

Mountain ridge
Mbadndàlì

Deep water
Làm

Open field/ grassfield
Ŋkà'

Ocean
Lìbà

Rain
Mbìŋ

Raindrop
Tabmbɨŋ

Ravine
Fen

River
Nchì

River bed
Kàŋnchì

Gravel
Ŋkwa'laŋ

Smoke
Njinjǐmu'

Sky /heaven
Nidəŋ

Star
Sàŋ

Steep slope
Ghəm

Rock
Wo

Storm /hurricane
Ntəŋkà'

Puddles/Potholes
Tìtămnchì

Valley
Bɔ̀'tì / fen

Waterfall
Vàvà

Raffia Vineyard
Nǎndù'

World
Mvi

Wave
Mba'nchì

Well or Spring
Sâ'nsi

Swamp
Nchə̀'

Whirlwind
Ŋgùlum

Sun
Nyùm

Desert
Lìbàŋkwa'laŋ

Fern
Tənnyìkɔ̀b

Birds
Bà Bɨsɨŋ

African hawk eagle
Lawum

Bannerman's turaco
Ngu'

Bee eater
Tâtɔ̀ŋ

Cattle egret
Mɨsɨ̂ŋ nyàm nchì

Bronze mannikin
Mɨja

Common cuckoo
Nchwèn

Common waxbill
Sĭsì

Crane (waterfowl)
Sɨŋchì

Crow
Ntăŋɔ̀

Dove
Mbuŋù

Duck
Ngôbnchì

Warbler
Tèŋkà'

Guinea fowl
Ngaŋsìŋ / Sɨŋgwè

Hawk
Chɔ'

Hen
Mâŋgɔb

Kingfisher
Sǎsàd

Laughing dove
Pădpâd

Nest
Nsa

Owl
Kùŋndɨ̀m

Partridge
Sɨŋgwè

Parrot
Kwăkùd

Pigeon
Mbuŋù

Quail
Ŋgɔbkɨ̀lɔg

Rooster
Ŋkɛ̀' ŋgɔb

Raven
Ntǎŋɔ̀

Sparrow
Mɨjikɔ̀d

Swallow
Pepè

Turtle dove
Mbuŋɨ̀kɔ̀b

Weaver bird
Nchô'bàŋ

Wood cock
Təmsɨŋ

Stone partridge
Təmsɨŋ

Woodpecker
Kɔkɔ'mbèntɨ

Starling
Njɔlɔŋmbɨ

Nightjar
Kukɔ̀ŋ

Dressing
Kĕ mà We'

Hand bag
Bămlèbbo

Bangle
Chaŋ

Belt
Kɔ̀b

Feathered hat used for dances
Chɔd

Button
Mbà'

Cap
Chǝ̌'tu

Cowrie
Mbɨm

Grassfield cap
Ŋkàb nswi'

Hat
Chǝ̌'tu

Head scarf
Kudtu

Ivory Bracelet
Lòŋ

Watch
Nyùm

Pearl necklace
Mfa

Ring
Wòbtì

Dress
Nji (generic for clothing)

Trousers
Sòŋkù

Type of necklace worn by men
Jàla

Shoes
Tab

Embroidered regalia for men with a smaller opening for the hands
Yadàla

Embroidered regalia for men with ample opening for the hands
Tɔghɨ

Sleeveless top for men with large open sides
Palìwà

Wool embroidered hat
Ndàb

Farm and Hunting
Ŋgwɛn boà Vum

Axe
Njàm

Bamboo
Ndèŋ

Beehive
Kɨkǎʼ dù

Bullet
Ŋkŏŋndìkàŋ

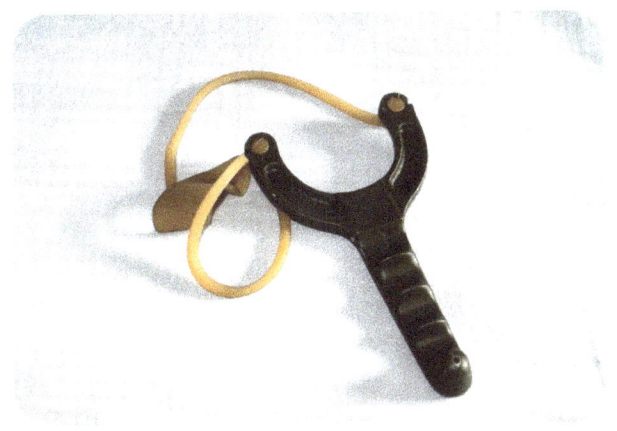

Catapult
Lòbàgôn

Earth worm
Nyàmlɔb

Elephant grass
Sùsùŋ

Farm
Ŋgwɛn / fà'

Flower
Ntɔlɔŋ

Garden
Ŋgwɛn

Grass
Ŋgə̀

Goat pen
Kădmbi

Gun
Ndìkàŋ

Gun powder
Fŭndìkàŋ

Hoe
So

Hut
Juŋ

Leaf
Fù

Mud
Tìtɔ̀b

Palm fronds
Vaŋ

Pig pen
Ŋkâ'kunyàm

Saddle
Lěŋ nyàmbà'nì

Scarecrow
Fàŋìŋkan

Seed
Ŋgɛ̀d yum

Slingshot
Ŋgìsàd

Soil
Ncha'

Stable
Ndânyàm

Sword
Minyîbɛ̀d

Tree
Tɨ

People
Bòn\Bɨ̀n

Man
Mɨmbàŋ

Woman
Mìŋgwi

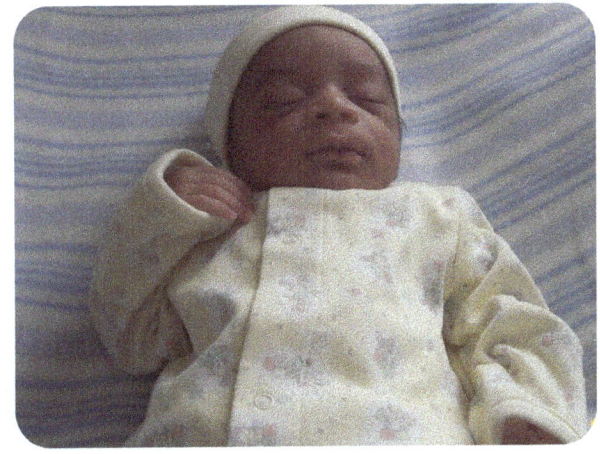

Baby
Mômbɔd

Child
Mon

Girl
Mômìŋwi

Boy
Mômumbàŋ

Doctor
Dɔktà

Children
Bon

Father
Ba

Mother
Nǎ

Bachelor
Ŋkɛ̀

Groom
Ndûŋgòndam

Bride
Ŋgòndam

Grandmother
Kǎ

Grandfather
Dǒ

King
Mfòn

Prince
Tìtà

Princess
Nìnà

Family
Ŋgə̀d

Music and Dance
Kě Wè boà Bɛn

Bamboo flute
Gà

Type of flute
Gàkwàn

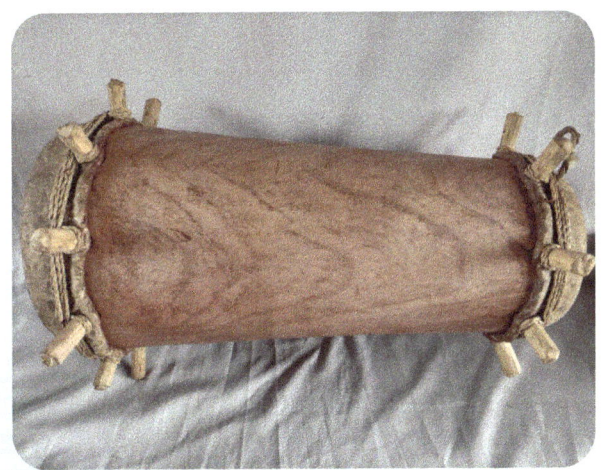

Double-headed arm drum
Yămà

End blown flute made from elephant tusk
Ntàŋ

Fiber tutu skirt
Nswi'

Finger harp
Luŋ

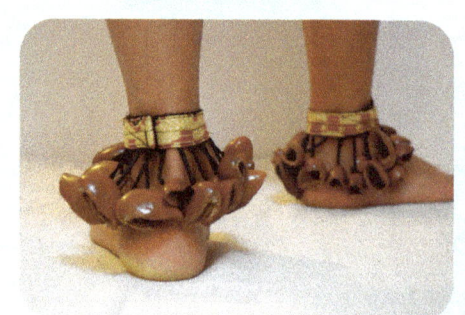
Fruit-shell rattle
Nděkùm

Gourd net rattle
Mbàchà'

Iron gong
Mìŋkəŋkəŋ

Horse tail
Saŋ

Xylophone
Njaŋ

Mask for dancing
Tukùm

Paired barrel drums
Bon Mbotà/Kòŋga

Rattle
Nchǎ'nchà'

Single-headed hourglass drum
Daŋgà

Slit gong
Ŋkɨ̀ndɨ̀ŋ

Large drum
Mâŋkà'

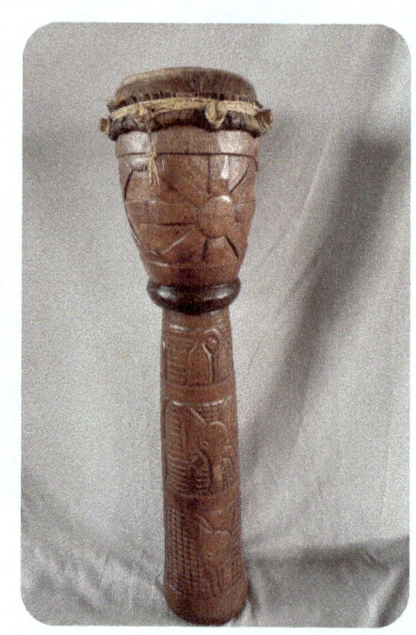

Long narrow drum
Fɔm

ADDITIONAL VOCABULARY

People

Friend / nsun
Husband / ndum
Widow / ŋku'
Widower / ŋku'
Wife / ŋgwi

Familial Relationships

Father / Ba
Paternal uncle / bâmbɔd (junior brother to the father) bâŋgukɛd (older brother of father)
Paternal aunt/ father's sister/ sister-in-law / Tăŋgwi
Sibling / mfɛd
Brother /mfɛd
Sister / mfɛd
Mother / nǎ
Maternal uncle / nimbàŋ
Maternal aunt / nǎmbɔd (*literal:* Mother's junior sister) nǎŋgukɛd (*literal:* mother's older sister)
Grandfather /dǒ
Grandmother /kǎ
Younger brother of grandfather /dǒmbɔd
Older brother of grandfather /dǒŋgukɛd
Cousin / mfɛd
Co-wife / mfu' (used in a polygamous marriage to refer to a fellow co-wife)
Mother-in-law of wife / madû
Mother-in-law of husband / ŋgɔm
Father-in-law of husband / chì (also son-in-law or brother-in-law)
Father-in-law of wife / tadû

Nephew & niece / Mɨnjàd/ daughter's children (called so by their grandfather). Also used to refer to the children of a man's sister. (bɨnjàd, pl)
Bridesmaid / fà'ndam
Young woman given to the first wife as a nurse maid who will be married later/ ndèbŋgòŋ

Parts of the body / mbùm

Ankle /mɨghə̂'kù
Bladder / ndâ nchèn
Bowels/ nto
Breast/nipple – bɨn
Buttocks / mbə'nì
Chest/ghàŋ
Chin / mbuŋchù
Coccyx / fə̀lə̀ŋchìŋnì
Ear / tuŋ
Elbow / jŭŋbo / ntŏŋbo
Eyeball /mbăŋli'
Eyes / mi'
Finger / sibo
Fingernails / ŋkimì
Midfoot / cha' kù
Groin / lə̀b
Hand /bo
Head / tu
Heart muscle / mbăŋntɨm
Heel / ntŏŋkù
Hipbone/ tubŭ'jəŋ
Hips / tubŭ'jəŋ
Kidney /mbăŋŋkòn
Knee joint / jŭŋkù
Large intestine / ndâmbɛd

Leg /kù
Lips/ kǔmnchù
Little finger / sibo ŋkə'
Liver/mbimɨ̀n
Lower leg / tăbkù
Lung/mbimbɔdkɛd
Mouth / nchù
Navel /tɔ̀ŋ
Nose / ŋkǒnji'
Palm / cha'bo /lanbo
Penis / kə̀d
Rib / kən ŋkwà'
Scrotum/nchàm
Shin/ ŋkɔŋmfɨn
Shoulder / sobo
Shoulder blade /gha'bo
Skull /wɔlɔ'tu
Skull bones / ghələŋ
Sole of foot / lankù
Spinal cord / kən ŋkwèn
Stomach / bɔm
Teeth /nsɔ̀ŋ
Testicles / mbăŋnchàm
Tip of the tongue/nchâlɨm
Throat/larynx /môtɔ̆ŋ
Thumb / sibô ŋgɨ
Toes /sikù
Tongue / lɨm
Upper arm /tû'bo
Uterus /ndâmon
Vagina / chə'
Vein /ŋgàŋ
Vertebrae/ kən ŋǎ' ŋkwèn
Waist / du'
Windpipe / ŋkɨ̌ môtɔ̀ŋ
Wrist / cha'nibo

Disease / jaŋ

Asthma / kàŋ
Boil / là̀b
Conjunctivitis / bàŋmi'
Diarrhea / kwǎbɔm
Dysentery / chə̆msi

Eczema / tàŋ
Goiter / tabtɔ̀ŋ
Hunchback / mbìsiŋ
Infertility / jɛn
Jigger / kôkù
Kind of syphilis / mɨchə̆dkə̀d
Leprosy / wònŋkə̀m
Mumps / ghə̀tighə̀'
Pneumonia / kĕbɨ̀ŋkɨ
Rash on the head /mbitì
Rheumatism / kwɛdnìkən or kwɛdnìmbùm
Skin disease which causes rashes / ŋgɨ̀làŋ
Sonambolism / tuŋu
Sterility/ fə̀d
Tape worm – ndɨm / nyɔ̆mnyòm

Time Periods/ ndìb

Today / ndî
Tomorrow / fɔmvi
Yesterday / Nì ŋkù'
Week / ŋgàb
Month / ŋu
Year /lùm
This year / yɔ lùm
Last year / lùm à kà lǎ a
New Year/ Lùm mfi
Fixed time / Ndìb ŋka ŋka

Parts of the Day

Morning / Nì mbǎ'mbà'
Morning around 9am / ndìb nyùm kɔ'ti a
Noon / ndìb nyùm baŋ a / ndìb nyùm tâm ŋdɔŋ a
Afternoon/ nì sà'
Afternoon around 3pm / ndìb nyùm swi a
Evening / ndìb nyùm bɔd a
Sunset / ndìb nyùm cho ma mbad a
Midnight / ghəghâ'ŋgɔ̀ŋ
Time when the moon goes down / nchônu

Cardinal points

East / ntûmnyùm
West / nchônyùm

Seasons and Time Period

Dry season / ndìblùm
Rainy season / ndìbmbìŋ
Holiday / ndìb fətì
Childhood / ndìb mbɔd
Yesteryears / ndìb kɨsɨ

Months of the year in Mubakɔ and some Mungaka descriptions

January / Sòja (lùm mfi / New Year)
February / Sònìa
March / Sòjela
April / Sŏduna
May / Sògàmba
June / Bolùwa
July / Sagwà'a (ŋu wom fà' nì so – farm bed making month)
August / Gwànsòa (ŋu kwàli ŋgwàfɨd – month of heaping soil around maize)
September / Sòsakèa
October / Vòmsòa (ŋu voma)
November / Sogeba (ŋu tă' ŋkwîn Lela/ Month to fetch firewood ŋu mà naŋ ŋkaŋ / month to prepare corn beer)
December / Lèsòa (ŋu Lela – Month of the Lela festival)
Sòsasìa (undetermined)

Days of the week (8-day week cycle)

Ŋgɔ'
Ndànsi
Ŋkɔ'ntan
Ntânbà'nì
Fòncham
Ntûmŋgwɛn
Ntânmbutu
Jɨ̆mbufûŋ

Vocations/Professions

Apiculturist (bee farmer) / Ŋgàŋ-tă'-dù
Architect / Ŋgàŋ-kàti-kǔmndab
Artist / ngàŋ-kàti
Astronomer / Ŋgàŋ-lɨ̆nsàŋ
Banker / Ŋgàŋ-kɨbti-ŋkab
Barber / Ŋgàŋ-kom-tu
Basket weaver / Ŋgàŋ-ba'-ŋkì'
Book seller / Ŋgàŋ-fɨ̌n-ŋwà'nì
Brewer / Ŋgàŋ-naŋ-ndù'
Bricklayer / Ŋgàŋ-bom-ncha'
Butcher / Ŋgàŋ-wǎd-nyàm
Carpenter / Ŋgàŋ-kom-tɨ
Cattle rearer / Ŋgàŋ-mǎ'-nyàm
Ceramist / Ŋgàŋ-bom-mbaŋ
Cobbler / Ŋgàŋ- lènti-tab
Cook or chef / Ŋgàŋ-naŋ-mbaŋ
Dancer / Ŋgàŋ-nyɨ̆ŋ-bɛn
Doctor/physician / Dɔktà
Driver / Ŋgàŋ-nɨ̆d-motò
Emissary / Ŋgàŋ-ntum
Farmer / Ŋgàŋ-fǎ'-ma-ŋgwɛn
Firefighter / Ŋgàŋ-və'ti-mu'
Fisherman / Ŋgàŋ-mǎ'-lɔb
Fortuneteller or diviner / Ŋgàŋ-fuŋ-ŋgam
Goat trader / Ŋgàŋ-fɨ̌nmbi
Grave digger / ŋgàŋ-tuŋ-tusì
Hair braider / Ŋgàŋ-ba'-tu
Hairdresser / Ŋgàŋ-nèbti- tu
Harpist or lute player / Ŋgàŋ-bu'-luŋ
Hornblower / Ŋgàŋ-tɔŋ-ndɔŋ
House builder / Ŋgàŋ-bom-ndab
Hunter / Ŋgàŋ-nya'-nyàm
Hunter / Ŋgàŋ-vum
Interpreter of language / Ŋgàŋ-bìti-chu
Judge / Ŋgàŋ- chăd sa' / Ŋgàŋ-sa'-sa'
Keeper of slaves / Ŋgàŋ-mǎ'-ŋkwàn
Lawmaker/legislator - Ŋgàŋ-nèbti-kàn
Lawyer / Ŋgàŋ-sa'-sa'
Mat weaver / Ŋgàŋ-ba'-kè
Magician/sorcerer / Mɨ̆sà
Mechanic / Ŋgàŋ-nèbti-motò
Merchant or trader / Ŋgàŋ-ntan
Messenger / Ŋgàŋ-ntum
Midwife / Ŋgàŋ-kə-vi
Musician or singer / Ŋgàŋ- jŏb-nchì
Painter / Ŋgàŋ-ta'ni-ndab
Palmwine tapper / Ŋgàŋ-lĕŋndù'
Pastor/chaplain / Ŋgàŋ-kiti-ŋkù'mɨ

Pharmacist /Ŋgàŋ-fĩn-fù
Philanthropist / Ŋgàŋ-kɔ̆ŋ-bòn
Philosopher / ŋgàŋ-kwà'ni-nŭ-mvi
Photographer / Ŋgàŋ-lɔ̆'-kà'à
Pilot /Ŋgàŋ-tă-tàkɨtɨ
Potter / Ŋgàŋ-bom-mbaŋ
Retailer/ Ŋgàŋ-fĩn-kĕ
Sailor / Ŋgàŋ-fă'ma-nchĭlìbà
Sheep shearer / Ŋgàŋ-bamti-nyŭŋ-njə̀mbi
Shepherd / Ŋgàŋ-beb-mbi
Slave trader /Ŋgàŋ-fĩnbòn / (traitor)
Soldier / Ŋgàŋ-mă'-bɛ̀d /sogè
Spy / Ŋgàŋ-nya'-ŋgɔ̀ŋ
Swimmer / Ŋgàŋ-wɔ'-nchì
Tailor/seamstress- Ŋgàŋ-ta-nji
Teacher/professor /Ŋgàŋ-na'ti-ŋwà'nì
Town clerk or secretary of state / Ŋgàŋ-ŋwà'ni-nŭŋgɔ̀ŋ
Translator of books/letters / Ŋgàŋ-bĭd-ŋwà'nì
Traveller / Ŋgàŋ-kŭjìd
Treasurer of the city/Minister of Finance/ Ŋgàŋ-kiti-ŋkab-ŋgɔ̀ŋ
Trumpeter / Ŋgàŋ-tɔŋ tàŋ
Warder / Ŋgàŋ-beb-ndâ-chaŋ
Workman / Ŋgàŋ-fà'
Writer/author / Ŋgàŋ-ŋwà'ni-ŋwà'nì

PHOTO CREDITS

African forest buffalo by H. Zell Wikicommons licensed under Creative Commons Attribution-Share Alike 3.0 Unported license.
Pygmy elephant by Shanka S. Wikicommons licensed under Creative Commons Attribution 2.0 Generic license.
Black winged kite Alejandro Bayer Tamayo Flickr
Stone partridge by Liki Fumei, licensed under Creative Commons Attribution-Share Alike 3.0 Unported license.
Common Cuckoo by Imran Shah licensed under Creative Commons Attribution-Share Alike 2.0 Generic license
Bannerman's Turaco by Jose Olivares Compres CC licensed under the Creative Commons Attribution-Share Alike 3.0 Unported
Spear grass by JMK
Weevil by CSIRO [CC BY 3.0 (http://creativecommons.org/licenses/by/3.0)], via Wikimedia Commons
Reedbuck: Yathin S Krishnappa CC by 3.0 https://creativecommons.org/licenses/by-sa/3.0/
Water snake: © Timothy Lewis | Dreamstime.com
Small black fox: © Tom Hansch | Dreamstime.com
Maggots: Ariya Shookh licensed under the Creative Commons Attribution-ShareAlike 4.0 License
African ground squirrel:© Mikhail Blajenov | Dreamstime.com
Talking drum: © Umehz Charles | Dreamstime.com
Black stinking bug by Katja Schulz licensed under the Creative Commons Attribution 2.0 Generic license.
Customs office: © Sonnenbergshots | Dreamstime.com
Bamun Sultan Palace: licensed under the Creative Commons Attribution-Share Alike 3.0 Unported license.
Cape gooseberry: © Jat306 |Dreamstime.com
Slingshot:©Yellow1972|Dreamstime.com
Field rat:©Kampan Butshi | Dreamstime.com
Laughing dove: Charles James Sharp - Own work, from Sharp Photography, sharpphotography, CC BY-SA 3.0, https://commons.wikimedia.org/w/index.php?curid=31334619
Whirlwind CC Ahlynka licensed under the Creative Commons Attribution-Share Alike 4.0 International license.
Corn beer pot (umqombothi): © Lucian Coman | Dreamstime.com
Bookshop: Ethan Doyle White at English Wikipedia Licensed under the Creative Commons Attribution-Share Alike 4.0 International license.
Shrew mouse: © Matthijs Kuijpers | Dreamstime.com
Reedbuck: David Castor, available under the Creative Commons CC0 1.0 Universal Public Domain Dedication
Photo of bathroom © Nuvisage | Dreamstime.com
Photo of bamboo courtesy of Aloysius Vutumu
Photo of palmwine jug courtesy of Tifuh Mbahzang
Photo of kalimba © Chaidir Fitriansyah | Dreamstime.com
Photo of xylophone © Ermess | Dreamstime.com
Photo 42869166 /African Princess © Matthias Ziegler | Dreamstime.com
Photo of cocoa tree 4672619 © Shariff Che Lah | Dreamstime.com
Photo of beef © Phrejphotos | Dreamstime.com
Bamenda Town: by Njeimosestimah, CC BY-SA 3. licensed under the Creative Commons Attribution-Share Alike 3.0 Unported license.
Egusi soup:© Ppy2010ha | Dreamstime.com
House cricket by Aiwok : licensed under the Creative Commons Attribution-Share Alike 3.0 Unported, 2.5 Generic, 2.0 Generic and 1.0 Generic license.
Locusts © Gall0wsraven | Dreamstime.com
Freckled nightjar (Caprimulgus tristigma) Charles J. Sharp - Own work licensed under the Creative Commons Attribution-Share Alike 4.0 International license.

INDEX

Achu coco 34
Achu soup 37
African cashew 29
African civet 43
African forest Buffalo 43
African ground squirrel 43, 89
African hawk eagle 62
African olive 34
African Plums 29
Afternoon 86
Agama lizard 43
Alligator pepper 34
Animal horn 44
Animals 38
Ankle 85
Ant 38
Antelope 44
Anvil hammer 2
Apiculturist 87
April 87
Architect 87
Armadillo 44
Artist 87
Asthma 86
Astronomer 87
August 87
author 88
Avocado 29
Axe 72

Baboon 45
Baby 77
Bachelor 78
Bambara groundnut 26
Bambara ground nut pudding 29
Bamboo 72
Bamboo flute 81
Bamboo stool 11
Banana leaf 30

Bangle 68
Banker 87
Bannerman's turaco 62
Barber 87
basket 4, 9, 13
Basket for carrying chicken 10. *See also* basket
Basket weaver 87
Bat 44
Bathroom 20
Beans 30
Bed 3
Bedroom 1
Bee 38, 62
Bee eater 62
Beehive 72
Beetle 38
Bell 22
Belt 68
Bicycle 24
Birds 62
Bitter kola 26
Bitterleaf 27
Black pepper 17
Bladder 85
Blanket 9
Boa constrictor 44
Boat 25
Boil 86
Book 21, 22, 87
Book cover 22
Book seller 87
Bookshop 20, 89
Bottle 8, 17
Bottle cover 8
Bowels 85
Bowl 12
Box 4
Boy 78
Bread 30

Breast 85
Brewer 87
Bricklayer 87
Bride 79, 85
Bridesmaid 85
Bridge 25
Bronze mannikin 63
Broom 4
Brother 85
Buffalo horn 45
Buildings 18
Bullet 72
Butcher 87
Butterfly 38
Buttocks 85
Button 69

Calabash 10, 17
Calabash for serving palmwine 10. *See also* calabash
Calabash used for tapping palmwine 10
Cameroon aframomum 34
Cameroon clawless otter 45
Camwood powder 7
can v, x, 1
Cane rat 46
Cap 69
Cape gooseberry 29, 89
Car 24
Cardinal points 87
Carpenter 87
Carrot 35
Cassava 30
Castor oil plant 35
Cat 45
Catapult 73
Caterpillar 39
Cattle egret 62

91

Cattle rearer 87
Cave 54
Ceiling 2
Ceramist 87
Chair 3
Chameleon 45
chaplain 88
chef 87
Chest 85
Chewing stick 7
Child 77
Childhood 87
Children 78
Chimpanzee 45
Chin 85
Christmas ix
Church ix, 18
Clay pot 12, 13
Clay Pot for brewing beer 12
Clay pot for cooking fufu 13
Clock 6
Cloud 54
Cluster yams 33
Cobbler 87
Cobweb 5
Coccyx 85
Cockroach 39
Cocoa 35
Cocoyam 27, 30
Cocoyam leaves 27
Coffee 30
Colocasia flower 37
Comb 2
Common cuckoo 63
Common waxbill 63
Conjunctivitis 86
Cook 87
Cooking 12
Cork 6
Corn 31, 36, 89
Corn flour 31
Corn fufu 36
Corn & groundnut pudding 36
Corn pudding 36
country 20
Country onions 31
Court 19
Cousin 85
Cow 27, 46
Co-wife 85
Cow pea leaves 27

Cowrie 69
Crane 63
Crescent 54
Crocodile 46
Cross 18
Crow 63
Cup 13
Curtain 6
Customs office 19, 89

Dance 81
Dancer 87
Days of the week 87
December 87
Deep water 57
Deer 49
Desert 61
Diarrhea 86
Dice 23
Disease 86
Doctor 78, 87
Dog 46
Door 5
Double-headed arm drum 81
Dove 63
Dragonfly 39
Dress 70
Dressing 68
Dried crayfish 31
Drink 13
Driver 87
Dry season 87
Duck 64
Dung beetle 39
Dust 54
Dwarf banana 28
Dysentery 86

Ear 85
Earth worm 73
East 87
Eczema 86
Egg 31
Egusi soup 37, 89
Elbow 85
Elephant 46, 73
Elephant grass 73
Embroidered regalia for men with ample opening for the hands 71
Embroidered regalia for men with a smaller opening for the hands 71
Emissary 87
End blown flute made from elephant tusk 81
Envelope 22
Evening 86
Eyeball 85
Eyes 85

Familial Relationships 85
Family 80
Farm 72, 73
Farmer 87
Father 78, 85
Father-in-law of husband 85
Father-in-law of wife 85
Feathered hat used for dances 68
February 87
Fermented corn porridge 36
Fern 61
Fiber tutu skirt 82
Field cricket 39
Field rat 47, 89
Fine sand 55
Finger 85
Finger harp 82
Fingernails 85
Firefighter 87
Firefly 40
Fireside 13
Firewood 13
Fish 47, 52
Fisherman 87
Fish otter 52
Fixed time 86
Flat basket for serving food 13
Flat calabash 14
Flower 73
Fly 40
Fog 55
Food 26
Footstool 11
Forest 55
Forest hog 49
Fork 14

Fortuneteller 87
Friend 85
Frog 47
Fruit-shell rattle 82
Funnel 15
Furniture 1

Gadfly 40
Garden 73
Garden eggs 27
Garden Huckleberry 28
Gift 11
Ginger 31
Girl 78
Gnome 6
Goat 47
Goat pen 74
Goat trader 87
Goiter 86
Gourd net rattle 82
Grandfather 79, 85
Grandmother 79, 85
Grass 74
grassfield 57
Grassfield cap 69
Grassfields ix, xi
Grasshopper 40
Grassland 55
Grave 19, 87
Grave digger 87
Gravel 58
Grinding stone 14
Groin 85
Groom 79, 85
Groundnut soup 36
Guava 28
Guinea corn 35
Guinea fowl 64
Gun 74
Gun powder 74

Hair braider 87
Hairdresser 87
Hand 85
Hand bag 68
Harpist 87
Hat 69
Hawk 64

Head 85
Head scarf 69
Heart muscle 85
heaven 59
Hedgehog 47
Heel 85
Helicopter 24
Hen 64
Hill 55
hill slope 56
Hipbone 85
Hippopotamus 48
Hips 85
Hoe 74
Hole 55
Holiday 87
Honey 32
Honeycomb 32
Hornblower 87
Horn cup 10
Horse 48
Horse tail 82
Hospital 19
House 1, 18, 43, 87, 89
House builder 87
House cricket 43, 89
Hunchback 86
Hunter 87
Hunting 72
hurricane 59
Husband 85
Hut 74
Hyena 48

Indian bamboo 9
Infertility 86
Insects 38
Interpreter of language 87
Iron gong 82
Ivory Bracelet 70

January 87
Jigger 86
Judge 87
July 87
June 87

Keeper of slaves 87
Key 3
Kid 50
Kidney 85
Kind of syphilis 86
King 80
Kingfisher 64
Knee joint 86
Knife 14
Kola nut 27

Ladder 7
Ladle 16
Lake 56
Lamp 3
Landscape 54
Large calabash for storing palm-wine 10
Large drum 84
Large intestine 86
Large taro root 37
Last year 86
Laughing dove 65
Lawmaker 87
Lawyer 87
Leaf 75
Leg 86
legislator 87
Leopard 48
Leprosy 86
Lice 40
Lightning 56
Lion 48
Lips 86
Little finger 86
Liver 86
Living room 1
Lizard 48
Locusts 41, 89
Long narrow drum 84
Lower leg 86
Lung 86
lute player 87

Maggot 41
Magician 87
Malanga 32
Man 77

March 87
Market 20
Mask for dancing 83
Mat 5, 87
Match sticks 14
Maternal aunt 85
Maternal uncle 85
Mat weaver 87
May 87
Meat 36
Mechanic 87
Medicine bag 8
Melon seeds 27
Merchant 87
Messenger 88
Midfoot 85
Midnight 86
Midwife 88
Millipede 41
Minister of Finance 88
Mirror 4
Money 10
Monkey 49
Month 86
Months of the year in Mubakɔ and some Mungaka descriptions 87
Moon 56
Morning 86
Mosquito 41
Moth 41
Mother 78, 85
Mother-in-law of husband 85
Mother-in-law of wife 85
Mountain 56
Mountain chain 56
Mountain peak 57
Mountain ridge 57
Mouse 49
Mouth 86
Mubako ix
Mud 75
Mumps 86
Mushroom 28
Music 81
Musician 88
Mygale blondi spider 41

Nail 5

Nature 54
Navel 86
Needle 5
Nephew 85
Nest 65
New Year 86
niece 85
Nightjar 67
Noon 86
Nose 86
November 87

Ocean 57
October 87
Okra 28
Older brother of grandfather 85
Open field 57
Owl 65
Ox 49

Painter 88
Paired barrel drums 83
Palm 86
Palm fronds 75
Palm kernel 17, 35
Palm kernel husks 17
Palm oil 15, 26
Palm oil fruits 26
Palm wine 32
Palmwine tapper 88
Paper 21
Parrot 65
Partridge 65
Parts of the body 85
Parts of the Day 86
Pastor 88
Paternal aunt 85
Paternal uncle 85
Peanut pudding 32
Peanuts 26
Pearl necklace 70
Pen 22
Pencil 22
Penis 86
People 77
Pepper 32
Pestle 15
Pharmacist 88

Philanthropist 88
Philosopher 88
Photo 3, 89
Photographer 88
physician 87
Pig 49
Pigeon 65
Pig pen 75
Pillow 9
Pilot 88
Places 18
Plane 24
Plantain porridge 37
Plantains 33
Plate 15
Pneumonia 86
Poisonous caterpillar 39
Porcupine 50
Pot 12, 15
Potatoes 33
Potholes 59
Potter 88
Prince 80
Princess 80
Prison 20
professor 88
Puddles 59
Pumice 2
Pumkin 28, 37
Pumkin leaves 28
Pygmy elephant 50
Python 50

Quail 66

Rabbit 50
Raffia palm fruit 29
Raffia Vineyard 60
Rag 7
Rain 57
Raindrop 58
Rainy season 87
Ram 46
Rash on the head 86
Rattle 83
Raven 66
Ravine 58
Razor 6

Red hot charcoal 12
Red palm weevil 50
Reedbuck 51
Retailer 88
Rheumatism 86
Rib 86
Rice 33
Ring 70
River 58
River bed 58
Road 25
Rock 59
Roof 2
Rooster 66
Royal antelope 51
Royal palace 19

Saddle 75
Sailor 88
Salt 33
Sawdust 16
Scarecrow 75
School 18, 21
School yard 21
Scissors 8, 22
Scrotum 86
seamstress 88
Seasons and Time Period 87
Seed 76
Seeds of peace 35
September 87
Sewing machine 8
Shad fish 51
Sheep 51
Sheep shearer 88
Shepherd 88
Shin 86
Shoes 71
Shoulder 86
Shoulder blade 86
Shrew mouse 44, 89
Sibling 85
Sieve 16
singer 88
Single-headed hourglass drum 83
Sister 85
sister-in-law 85
Skin disease which causes rashes 86

Skull 86
Skull bones 86
Sky 59
Slave trader 88
Sleeveless top for men with large open sides 71
Slingshot 76
Slit gong 83
Small basket 9. *See also* basket
Small beetles 40
Small black fox 51
small fish 52
Small grasshopper 43
Small stone for grinding 14
Small winged ant 42
Smoke 58
Snail 51
Snake 52
Soap 5
Soil 76
Soldier 88
Sole of foot 86
Sonambolism 86
Sparrow 66
Spider 42
Spinal cord 86
Spoon 16
Spring 60
Spy 88
Squirrel 52
Stable 76
Star 59
Starling 67
Steep slope 59
Sterility 86
Stick for cooking fufu 16
Stink bug 42
Stomach 86
Stone partridge 67
Stool 11
Storm 59
Students 23
Sugar cane 33
Sun 61
Sunset 86
Swallow 66
Swamp 61
Swimmer 88
Sword 76

Table 7
tadpole 52
Tailor 88
Tape worm 86
Taro root 34
Teacher 88
Teeth 86
Telephone 11
Termite 42
Testicles 86
This year 86
Thread 9
Throat/larynx 86
Thumb 86
thunder 56
Time Periods 86
Time when the moon goes down 86
Tin 1
Tip of the tongue 86
Toad 52
Tobacco leaves 34
Tobacco pipe 8
Today 86
Toes 86
Toilet 4
Tomorrow 86
Tong 17
Tongue 86
Toothbrush 8
Tortoise 52
Towel 9
Town 20, 88, 89
Town clerk or secretary of state 88
Toy 3
trader 87
Traditional gate 20
Translator of books 88
Transportation 24
Traveller 88
Treasurer of the city 88
Tree 76
Trousers 70
Trumpeter 88
Turtle dove 66
Type of flute 81
Type of necklace worn by men 71

Umbrella 7
Upper arm 86
Uterus 86

Vagina 86
Valley 60
Vein 86
Vertebrae 86
Vocations/Professions 87

Waist 86
Wall 6
Warbler 64
Warder 88
Wasp 42
Watch 70
Water 16, 53, 89
Waterbuck 53
Waterfall 60
waterfowl 63

Water snake 53
Wave 60
Weaver bird 67
Week 86
Weevil 42, 89
Well 60
West 87
Wheel 25
Whip 11
Whirlwind 61
White field mouse 53
Widow 85
Widower 85
Wife 85
Wild boar 49
Window 4
Windpipe 86
Woman 77
Wood ash 17
Wood cock 67
Wooden hammer 2
Woodpecker 67
Wood worm 53

Wool embroidered hat 71
Workman 88
Workplace 19
World 60
Wrist 86
Writer 88

Xylophone 83

Yams 34
Year 86
yellow soup 37. *See also* Achu soup
Yesterday 86
Yesteryears 87
Younger brother of grandfather 85
Young woman given to the first wife as a nurse maid who will be married later 85

www.ingramcontent.com/pod-product-compliance
Lightning Source LLC
Chambersburg PA
CBHW051358110526
44592CB00023B/2874